# PETERHOF

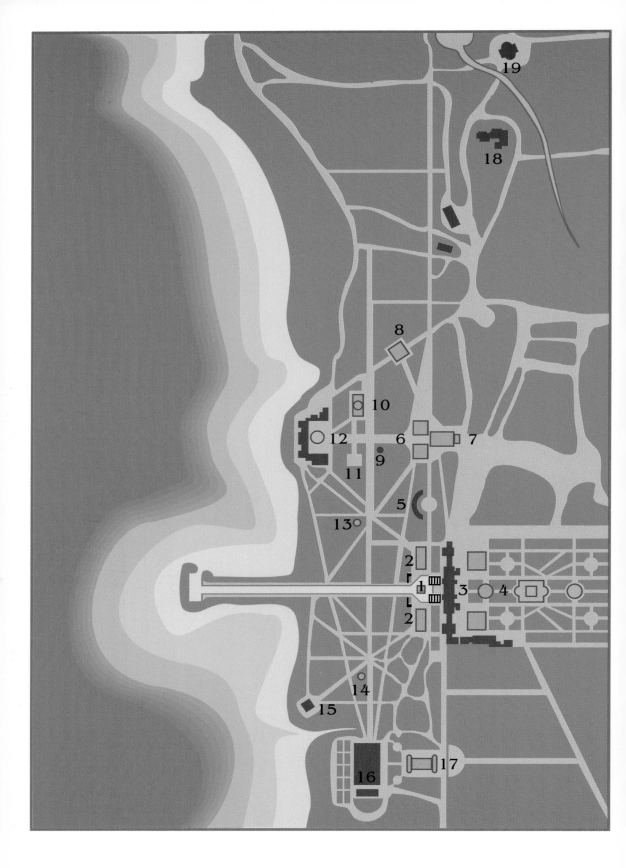

1. Fontains of the Great Cascade and *Samson Tearing Apart the Lion's Jaws Group*
2. *Bowl* Fountains
3. Great Palace
4. Upper Garden
5. Conservatory Pavilion and *Triton* Fountain
6. Roman Fountains
7. *Chessboard Hill* Cascade
8. *Pyramid* Fountain
9. Monument to Peter I (the Great)
10. *Sun* Fountain
11. Western Birdhouse
12. Monplaisir Palace
13. *Eve* Fountain
14. *Adam* Fountain
15. Pavilion Hermitage
16. Château de Marly
17. *Golden Hill* Cascade
18. Farm Palace
19. Cottage Palace

1. Fontänen der Großen Kaskade und Skulpturgruppe *Samson, der dem Löwen den Rachen aufreißt*
2. Fontänen Schalen
3. Großes Schloß
4. Oberer Garten
5. Pavillon Orangerie und Fontäne *Triton*
6. Römische Fontänen
7. *Schachbrettberg* (Drachen-Kaskade)
8. Fontäne *Pyramide*
9. Denkmal Peters I
10. Fontäne *Sonne*
11. Westvoliere
12. Schloß Monplaisir
13. Fontäne *Eva*
14. Fontäne *Adam*
15. Pavillon Ermitage
16. Schloß Marly
17. Marly-Kaskade *(Goldener Berg)*
18. Farmerpalast
19. Sommerpalast Cottage

1. Fontaines de la Grande Cascade et le groupe sculpté *Samson, déchirant la gueule du lion*
2. Fontaines-*Coupes*
3. Grand Palais
4. Jardin Supérieure
5. Pavillon-Orangerie et la Fontaine *Triton*
6. Fontaines Romaines
7. Cascade *La Montagne de l'Echiquier*
8. Fontaine *La Pyramide*
9. Monument à Pierre le Grand
10. Fontaine *Le Soleil*
11. Volière d'Ouest
12. Palais de Monplaisir
13. Fontaine *Eve*
14. Fontaine *Adam*
15. Pavillon l'Ermitage
16. Palais de Marly
17. Cascade *La Montagne d'or*
18. Palais de fermier
19. Palais de Cottage

# PETERHOF

## PALACES · PARKS · FOUNTAINS

ABRIS
Saint-Petersburg
1995

**Front of the cover:**
View of the Marine Canal
from the Portrait Gallery.
Blick aus dem Porträtsaal
auf den See-Kanal.
Vue de la Salle des Portraits
sur le Canal Maritime.

**Back of the cover:**
Château de Marly. View from
the Gulf of Finland.
Blick auf das Schloß Marly vom
Finnischen Meerbusen.
Palais de Marly. Vue du côté
du golfe.

RUSSIAN TEXT BY NINA VERNOVA
PHOTOS BY NATALIA AND KONSTANTIN DOKA
DESIGN BY VASILY BERTELS

Editor of the Russian text
Sergey Mikheev

Translated from the Russian
by Elena Vdovina, Tatjana Tsapalina,
Kira Golubeva, Maria Zakharova

**This edition was supported
by the State Museum
of Peterhof**

# THE GREAT PALACE

The marble column near the fence of the Upper Park of Peterhof bears the figure 29. This is the distance in kilometers from St Petersburg to the former marvelous country residence of the Russian Emperors, now the world famous park and palace museum ensemble.

The idea to create a residence as luxurious as the famous Versailles in France came to Peter I in 1714. The Emperor himself managed the design of the palace, parks and fountains. The French ambassador H. de Campredon wrote to Louis XV, that the rate of the building work of the residence was striking and amazing. The openning ceremony of Peterhof was held on 15 August, 1723. By that time some fountains were already operating, the Upper Chambers had been decorated, and the Hermitage Pavilion practically finished. The construction of the whole ensemble lasted for two centuries. The most prominent architects took part in the work - Jean Baptiste Le Blond, Niccolo Michetti, Bartolomeo Francesco Rastrelli, Juri Velten, Andrej Stakenschneider.

The structural centre of the ensemble is the Great Palace erected on the edge of a sixteen metre high terrace. The three-storey brick building with the elements of the former Upper Chambers in its central part was built in 1755 according to Bartolomeo Rastrelli's design. Later redecorations by Juri Velten mainly affected the Palace interiors and were due to the change of the baroque style by a new one - classical.

The Peterhof Great Palace was the official summer residence of the Russian Emperors. Its halls witnessed many important events, receptions and festivals, balls and masquerades housing up to three thousand guests at a time. The entrance to the Great Palace is from the Upper Garden. The luxu-

# GROßES SCHLOß

In den marmornen Obelisken am Gitter des *Oberen Gartens* ist die Zahl 29 eingemeinelt. Sie gibt die Entfernung zwischen Sankt-Petersburg und der prächtigen Sommerresidenz der russischen Zaren an, die heutzutage als Park- und Schloßensemble Peterhof weltbekannt ist.

Das Vorhaben eine Residenz zu bauen, die dem berühmten französischen Versailles nicht nachstehen soll, entstand unter Peter I. im Jahre 1714. Der Zar leitete persönlich die Projektierung von Schlössern, Parks und Springbrunnen. Der französische Botschafter H. de Campredon schrieb an Louis XV., daß die Errichtung dieser Residenz überraschend schnell voran gehe.

Schon am 15. August 1723 fand die feierliche Einweihung von Peterhof (Hof von Peter) statt. Mehrere Springbrunnen waren bereits in Betrieb, die Oberen Gemächer schon eingerichtet, fast fertig war die Ermitage, vollendet waren die Schlösser *Marly* und *Monplaisir*. Sämtliche Bauarbeiten an den Parkanlagen dauerten insgesamt zwei Jahrhunderte lang. Daran beteiligten sich berühmte Architekten wie Le Blond, Niccolo Michetti, Bartolomeo Francesco Rastrell, Juri Velten und Andrej Stakenschneider.

Das architektonische Zentrum des Ensembles ist das große Schloß, das sich am Rand der sechzehn Meter hohen natürlichen Terrasse erhebt. Das dreigeschossige Gebäude, das in seinem mittleren Teil einige Elemente der alten Oberen Gemächer einschließt, wurde nach dem Entwurf von Bartolomeo Francesco Rastrelli im Jahre 1755 errichtet. Spätere Veränderungen, die von Juri Velten hauptsächlich bei der Gestaltung des Interieurs vorgenommen wurden, widerspiegelten den

# LE GRAND PALAIS

Le chiffre 29 sur gravé l'obélisque de marbre érigé près de l'enceinte du Jardin Supérieur de Peterhof marque la distance en kilomètres qui sépare Saint-Pétersbourg d'une brillante résidence d'été des empereurs russes, aujourd'hui l'ensemble de palais et de parcs mondialement connu.

En 1714 Pierre le Grand eut l'idée de créer une résidence qui égalerait à fameux Versailles. L'empereur participait personnellement à la création des projets des fontaines, des palais et des parcs. L'ambassadeur français H. de Campredon écrivit à Louis XV que la rapidité des travaux était étonnante et même frappante.

L'inauguration de Peterhof ('le palais de Pierre' en hollandais) eut lieu le 15 août 1725. A ce moment-là plusieurs fontaines fonctionnaient déjà, le Palais Supérieur, les Palais de Monplaisir et de Marly furent bâtis; l'Ermitage fut achevé dans ses grandes lignes. La construction de l'ensemble dura deux siècles. Les architectes illustres y ont pris participation: J. -B. Leblond, B. F. Rastrelli, N. Michetti, I. Felten, A. Stakenschneider.

Le centre de l'ensemble est presenté par le Grand Palais, qui se dresse au bout d'une terrasse de 16 mètres. L'édifice de pierre à deux étages fondé sur le vieux Palais Supérieur fut érigé d'après le projet de B. F.Rastrelli. Des modifications postérieures faites par I.Felten touchaient principalement les intérieurs du Palais et témoignaient de l'événement du style classique. Aux XVIIIme - XIXme ss. le Grand Palais était une résidence officielle d'été des empereurs russes. Beaucoup d'événements importants eurent lieu dans ses salles, on y fit des fêtes et des accueilles, des bals et des mascarades. Elles pouvaient recevoir près de 3 mille invités à la fois.

1

rious gilt staircase leads to the no less marvelous Dance Hall which is the first of the palace gala rooms. Next is the Cheshma Room with 12 paintings by the German artist Philippe Hackert to commemorate the victory the Russian navy over the Turkish fleet in Cheshma Bay in June 1770. The theme of the Cheshma victory is continued in the adjacent Throne Room decorated with four large sea-scapes by the English painter Richard Paton. The symbols of marine glory are very much appropriate in Peterhof as its founder was also the creator of the Russian fleet.

The Throne Hall is the largest in the palace, designed for official receptions. All the elements of its décor, the dimensions, the light streaming through 28 two-tier windows, the abundance of mirrors, the fine design of the parquet floor, the portraits of Peter I and his family, were to signify the importance of the room among other marvelous halls of the palace. The main accent of the decoration is given to the wall behind the throne which is said to have belonged to Peter I.

A portrait of Catherine II on horseback is above the throne.

The small Audience Hall was not affected by later redecorations and has conserved the wonderful baroque décor of the middle of the 18th century and the plafond illustrating Torquato Tasso's poem *Jerusalem Delivered*. It is still stunning visitors with its glittering décor and variety of carved elements.

The White Dining Hall designed for official dinners is decorated in the style of classicism and produces the impression of calmness and peace in contrast with the luxury and splendour of the Audience Hall. Light tint prevails here, no painting is used, it is substituted by the wall bas-reliefs on the subjects of Greek mythology. There, on display, is a porcelain dinner set of 196 pieces

Stilwechsel vom Barock zum Klassizismus. *Großes Schloß* war eine offizielle Sommerresidenz der russischen Zaren. Hier wurden viele Feste und Empfänge, Bälle und Maskeraden abgehalten, zu denen bis zu dreitausend Gästen begrüßt wurden.

Der Eingang in das Schloß befindet sich auf der dem Oberen Garten zugewandten Seite. Die Paradetreppe mit dem vergoldeten Geländer führt in den prächtig gestalteten Tanzsaal, einen der Paradesäle des Schlosses. Dahinter liegt der *Tschesme-Saal*.

Die Wände dieses Saales schmücken zwölf Gemälde des deutschen Malers Philippe Jacob Hackert. Sie bilden eine künstlerische Chronik über den Sieg der russischen Flotte in der Tschesme-Bucht. Eine hervorragende Ergänzung zur Tschesme-Suite von Hackert sind vier riesengröße Gemälde von dem englischen Meister Richard Paton, die sich im Thronsaal befinden. Alle diese Gemälde sind Symbole des russischen Ruhmes. Sie passen besonders nach Peterhof, das unter Peters I., dem Gründer der russischen Flotte, erbaut wurde.

*Der Thronsaal* ist der größte Saal im Schloß, hier fanden gewöhnlich offizielle Empfänge statt. Die Größe des Saales, seine zahlreichen Spiegel, die ausgeprägte Zeichnung des Parketts, die Porträts von Peter I. und seiner nächsten Verwandten unterstützen die besondere Bedeutung dieses Raumes. Der festliche Eindruck dieses Saales entsteht auch durch das Licht, das durch die achtundzwanzig in zwei übereinanderliegenden Reihen angeordneten Fenster hereinströmt. Den gestalterischen Hauptakzent legte man auf die Ostwand, vor der der Thronsessel stand. Über dem Thronsessel hängt das große Reiterporträt Katharina II., eine Arbeit des dänischen Malers Virgilius Erichsen. Der Thronsessel soll Peter I. gehört haben.

Der kleine *Audienz-Saal* ist mit dem Plafond von dem italienischen Maler Paolo Ballarini geschmückt. Das Thema der Deckenbemalung wurde aus dem Poem *Das befreite Jerusalem* von Torquato Tasso genommen. Der Saal wurde späteren Veränderungen nicht unterzogen, ihm blieb die prächtige Barock-Gestaltung aus der Mitte des 18. Jahrhunderts erhalten. Auch heute überrascht er den

L'entrée du Grand Palais est située du côté du Jardin Supérieur. Le magnifique escalier doré mène dans la Salle de bal, aussi splendide, la première des salles d'apparat. La salle suivante est la Salle de Tchesmé. Les toiles du célèbre peintre allemand Ph.Hackert représentent la victoire navale de la Russie sur la flotte turque pendant la bataille à la baie de Tchesmé constituent sa décoration essentielle. Ce sujet est élaboré dans les quatre grands tableaux de R. Paton consacrés à la victoire de Tchesmé et situés dans la salle suivante - la Salle du Trône. Ces symboles de la gloire navale de la Russie sont bien à propos à Peterhof dont le fondateur était aussi le fondateur de la flotte russe.

La Salle du Trône est la plus vaste salle du Palais, la salle de grandes réceptions. Ses dimensions, les flots de lumière qui pénétrent dans la salle par 28 fenêtres, 12 lustres splendides, l'abondance de miroirs, la peinture de parquet, les portraits de Pierre le Grand et de ses parents proches - tout souligne l'importance de cette salle. Accent principal du décor est porté sur le mur devant lequel était placé le trône. C'est ici que l'on suspendit un grand portrait équestre de Catherine II peint par l'artiste danois V.Erichsen. La légende veut que ce trône ait appartenu à Pierre.

La petite Salle d'audiences dont le plafond peint par l'artiste italien P. Ballarini qui prit le sujet du poème de T. Tasse *La Jérusalem délivrée* ne subit pas de modifications postérieures et garde une garniture magnifique du style baroque du XVIIIme s. Son décor d'or et des éléments sculptés variés frappent les spectateurs.

Après la somptuosité et le brillant de la Salle d'audience la Salle à manger blanche où avaient lieu les dines de gala donne l'impression de sérénité et de calme. Elle fut décorée par I.

made by the English ceramist Josiah Wedgwood to the order of Catherine II in the 1760s; and Bohemian glassware of the 18th century. Another dinner set and large cobalt china vases painted with gold are displayed in the Great Blue Drawing Room which used to be the place for family dinners and is in the far end of the suite of rooms.

The rooms making up the women's wing of the palace - the Boudoir, the Bedroom, the Dressing Room, the Empress' Study as well as some official rooms such as the Imperial Standard Chamber, the Cavalier Chamber and the Secretary Room, are interesting thanks to their collections of pieces of art and interior décor.

A special impression is produced by the wall lining with ornamented satins. The Boudoir, lined with Lyon silk with partridges in the grass, was called the Partridge Drawing Room.

Most attractive are two Chinese Studies - the Eastern and Western ones. The lacquered wall panels, the ceiling plafonds and the parquet floor ornaments of precious wood species, the elaborated design of the tiled stoves and furniture cloth, the carving and collection of Chinese and Japanese porcelain and enamels - all invite one to the exotic world of distant and mysterious lands.

The central part of the palace is occupied by the hall with windows looking over the parterre of the Upper Garden on one side and the terrace of the Lower Park on the other. This is the former Upper Chambers preserved by B.Rastrelli. In the time of Peter I this hall was the main one in the palace. Later, 368 paintings by the Italian artist Pietro Rotari were placed there and the hall was called the Portrait Gallery. This historical part of the palace also houses the famous Oak Study of Peter I. The decoration of the first quarter of the 18th century by Le Blond has been

Besucher durch seinen glänzenden Dekor und die Mannigfaltigkeit seiner plastischen Elemente.
Im Unterschied zu dem Glanz und der Pracht des *Audienz-Saales* zeichnet sich der im klassizistischen Stil eingerichtete Speisesaal durch die feine harmonische Klarheit der Gestaltung aus. Der Saal diente für festliche Mahlzeiten. Hier herrschen helle
Töne vor, es fehlt die Malerei. Für den zierlichen Dekor des Saales wurden Basreliefs auf Sujets der antiken Mythen verwendet. Im Speisesaal wird das 196-teilige Service ausgestellt, das im Auftrag von Katharina II. in der englischen Fayencefabrik Wedgwood angefertigt worden ist. Hier steht auch Geschirr aus bohemischem Glas aus dem 18. Jahrhundert. Ein Bankettservice und größe mit Gold bemalte blaue Porzellanvasen sind im *Großen Blauen Speisezimmer* zu sehen. Dieser Speiseraum befindet sich am anderen Ende der Zimmerflucht und war für die Familienmahlzeiten bestimmt.
Die Zimmerflucht, die den Frauenteil des Schlosses einschließt: Boudoir, Schlafzimmer, Ankleidezimmer, das Kabinett der Zarin sowie die Dienstzimmer: Standartenzimmer, Kavalier-Zimmer, Sekretär-Zimmer, sind vor allem durch ihre Ausstattung und die sich in diesen Räumen befindlichen Sammlungen sehenswert. In der dekorativen Gestaltung dieses Interieurs fällt die Bespannung der Wände mit dem verschiedenartig gemusterten Stoff auf. Die Lyoner Seide mit der Abbildung der goldbraunen Rebhühner verschaffte dem Boudoir den Namen *Rebhuhngastzimmer*.
Zwei *Chinesische Kabinette* - das *Östliche* und *Westliche* - erregen immer die Aufmerksamkeit der Besucher. Die schwarzen chinesischen Lackpanneaus an den Wänden, bemalte Decken, das Parkett aus wertvollen Holzarten, keramische Öfen mit verschnörkeltem Muster, Stoffe, geschnitzte Möbel sowie eine chinesische und japanische Porzellansammlung versetzen die Besucher in die Exotik rätselhafter Länder.
In dem zentralen Teil des Schlosses, in den von Rastrelli gestalteten Oberen Gemächern, befindet sich der weiträumige doppellichtige Saal. Seine Fenstertüren auf der einen Seite führen

Felten dans le style classique. Des couleures claires dominent ici, la peinture est remplacée par des moulures en bas-reliefs sur des sujets mythologiques. On y voit exposé le service à 196 pièces réalisé par le céramiste britannique J.Wedgwood sur la commande de Catherine la Grande. Encore un service de gala et deux grands vases de porcelaine, peints d'or et de cobalt se trouvent au Grand salon bleu qui servait de salle à manger privée pour des repas famillials et qui est située de l'autre côté de l'enfilade.
Une enfilade de pièces qui compose l'appartement de l'impératrice du Palais: boudoir, chambre à coucher, cabinet de toilette, cabinet de l'impératrice et une série de pièces de service: salle d'étendards, salle des gardes, secrétariat - est intéressante avant tout par la décoration et les collections d'art. La force d'expréssion particulière de ces salles est dûe à la tapisserie des murs tendus de satin à peinture variée (la soie lyonnaise aux perdrix donna le deuxième nom au boudoir - Salon aux perdrix).
Deux Cabinets Chinois - d'Est et d'Ouest attirent constamment l'attention des visiteurs. Les panneaux laqués aux murs, les plafonds couverts de peintures, le parquet en marqueterie du bois précieux, les poêles de céramique aux dessins fantasques, les tissus, les meubles sculptés, la collection de porcelaine chinoise et japonaise, les émals - tout cela introduit dans le monde ·exotique des pays lointains et énigmatiques.
Dans la partie centrale du Palais on découvre une salle à deux lumières dont les fenêtres donnent sur le parterre du Jardin Supérieur et sur la terrasse du Parc Inférieur. A l'époque de Pierre le Grand c'était la salle principale du Palais. Après on y installa 368 tableaux du peintre italien P.

largely preserved. The study walls are covered with oak panels carved after Nicolas Pineau's drawings, the French sculptor and decorator, on subjects devoted to arts and sciences.

The Oak Staircase with nicely decorated cut railings leads downstairs.

The portrait of Peter I in a rich oak framing is another reminder of the great reformer of Russia and the founder of St Petersburg and Peterhof.

auf den *Oberen Garten* und auf der an-deren Seite auf die Terrasse des *Unteren Parks*. In der Zeit Peters I. diente er als Paradesaal. Später wurde der Saal mit 368 Bildern des italienischen Malers Pietro Potari ausgestattet, so daß er fortan als Porträtsaal oder Gemäldesaal bezeichnet wurde.

In diesem historischen Teil liegt auch das berühmte *Eichenholzkabinett* Peters I., Seine von Le Blond ausgeführte Ausstattung aus dem ersten Viertel des 18. Jahrhunderts ist bis heute erhalten geblieben. Das Kabinett ist mit Eichenholzpanneaus dekoriert. Sie wurden nach den Zeichnungen des französischen Bildhauers und Dekorateurs Nicolas Pineau gefertigt und verherrlichen die Wissenschaften und Künste. Eine Eichentreppe mit dem kunstvoll geschnitzten Geländer führt aus diesem Kabinett nach oben. An einer Wand hängt in einem prachtvoll geschnitzten Rahmen ein Porträt Peters I., so daß der Besucher noch einmal an den großen Reformer Rußlands, den Gründer von Petersburg und Peterhof, erinnert wird.

Rotari et la salle prit le nom de Salle des tableaux.

Dans cette partie historique se trouve le célèbre Cabinet de chêne de Pierre le Grand. Il conserve en général la décoration du premier quart de XVIIIme s. réalisé par J.-B. Leblond.

Le Cabinet est orné de panneaux de chêne exécutés d'après les dessins du peintre français N.Pineau. Leurs sujets glorifient les sciences et les arts.

Un escalier de chêne à la rampe fin ouvragée mène du Cabinet de chêne. Sur le mur on voit un portrait de Pierre le Grand en cadre de chêne richement decoré qui fait penser encore une fois au grand réformateur de la Russie, fondateur de Saint-Pétersbourg et Peterhof.

1. Great Palace. View from the Marine Canal.

Großes Schloß.
Blick vom See-Kanal.

Grand Palais.
Vue du Canal Maritime.

**3.** Cheshma Hall.
Tschesme-Saal.
Salle de Tchesmé.

▷
**4.** Throne Hall.
Thronsaal.
Salle du Trône.

**2.** Gala Staircase.
Paradetreppe.
Escalier d'honneur.

**5.** Audience Hall.

Audienz-Saal.

Salle d'audience.

**6.** Clock *Apollo's Chariot*. Bronze, jasper, gilt. Sculptor P.-Ph.Thomire. France. End of the 17th century.

Uhr *Kampfwagen Apollos.* Bronze, Jaspis, vergoldet. Bronzeschmied P.-Ph.Thomire. Frankreich. Ende des XVII.

Pendule: *Char d'Apollon.* Bronze doré, jaspe. Sculpteur P.F.Thomire. France. Fin du XVIIe s.

**7.** White Dining Room.

Weißer Speisesaal.

Salle à manger blanche.

**9.** Western Chinese Study.
Westliches Chinesisches Kbinett.
Cabinet Chinois d'Ouest.

**8.** Northern Suite of Rooms.
View from the Western Chinese Study.

Nördliche Zimmerflucht.
Blick aus dem Westlichen Chinesischen
Kabinett.

Enfilade Nord. Vue du Cabinet Chinois
d'Ouest.

**10.** Eastern Chinese Study.

Östliches Chinesisches Kabinett.

Cabinet Chinois d'Est.


**11.** Northern Suite of Rooms.
View from the Eastern Chinese Study.

Nördliche Zimmerflucht.
Blick aus dem Östlichen Chinesischen
Kabinett.

Enfilade Nord.
Vue du Cabinet Chinois d'Est.

**12.** Cavalier Chamber.

Kavalierzimmer.

Salle des gardes.

**13.** Blue Drawing Room. Banquet Set.
Imperial Porcelain Factory.
Russia. 1848-1853.

Blaues Empfangszimmer. Bankettservice.
Kaiserliche Porzellanmanufaktur.
1848-1853.

Salon bleu. Service de gala.
Usine Impériale de porcelaine.
Russie. 1848-1953.

**14.** Blue Drawing Room.

Blaues Empfangszimmer.

Salon bleu.

**16.** Oak Study of Peter the Great.
Eichenholzkabinett Peters I.
Cabinet de chêne de Pierre le Grand.

**15.** Oak Staircase.
Eichentreppe.
L'escalier de chêne.

# THE LOWER PARK AND THE UPPER GARDEN

The view of the Lower Park and the sea from the terrace before the Great Palace is unforgetable. The Great Cascade shines with its gilt sculptures and silver fountain sprays in the centre. It is the principal structure of the grandiose fountain system of Peterhof. The main idea of the Peterhof ensemble to commemorate the glorious victories of Russia during the fight for the access to the Baltic was symbolically expressed in its design.

It was not by chance that Peter I chose this locality for his country residence. In the course of the survey of local hills several ponds vere found to be fed by ground water springs 20 km to the South of Peterhof. In 1721 the duct system was designed for the water to run into the collectors of the Upper Garden, by gravity, and then to the Lower Park to raise the multilple jets of its fountains.

The layout of the Great Cascade was worked out by Peter I. He could see the Grotto, the Balustrade, the first bas-reliefs and mascarons built and 12 allegoric fugures and decorative vases cast in Holland. After Peter's death his ideas continued to be realized. The two-figure statue of Tritons blowing the trumpet designed by B.Rastrelli was mounted. Many statues cast after classical originals were added to the Cascade. The Basket-fountain is in front of the Grotto. It is formed by 28 criss-crossed jets around a huge basin. There are five four-tier cascades of white marble on each side of the terrace.

The most powerful fountain of Peterhof is Samson, placed in the centre of the reservoir, before the Great Cascade. The decision to build this fountain was made in 1734 when the 25th anniversary of the Russian victory over the Swedes at Poltava was celebrated. The huge hero Samson, cast in bronze, is tearing apart the

# OBERER GARTEN UND UNTERER PARK

Von der Terrasse an der Nordfassade des Großen Schlosses aus hat der Besucher einen herrlichen Blick auf den Unteren Park und das Meer. In der Mitte ist die Große Kaskade, die durch zahlreiche vergoldete Plastiken und silbrige, gen Himmel emporschießende Wasserstrahlen der Fontäne überrascht. Die Große Kaskade ist die zentrale Anlage des grandiösen Fontänensystems Peterhofs. Darin fand die Hauptidee des Peterhofs Ensembles ihre Verwirklichung - die Verherrlichung der Siege Rußlands im Kampf um den Zugang zur Ostsee.

Peter I. Wählte nicht zufällig diese Gegend für seine Residenz. Auf den von Peterhof unweit entfernten Höhen - 22 km südlicher - entdeckte man Wasserbehälter, die von unterirdischen Wasserquellen gespeist wurden. Das natürliche Gefälle des Geländes von den Ropschaer Quellen zum Meer ausnutzend, wurde ein hydrotechnisches selbstfließendes System gebaut. Das Wasser sammelte sich in Reservoirs und strömte dann durch Röhren nach unten und stieg danach gewaltig in zahlreichen Wasserspielen und Springbrunnen des Unteren Parks auf.

Die Idee der Komposition der Großen Kaskade stammt von Peter I. Schon zu seiner Lebzeit entstanden die Grotte und die Balustrade. Es erschienen die ersten Basreliefs und Maskarone.

In Holland ließ man 12 allegorische Figuren und dekorative Vasen angefertigen. Nach dem Tod Peters I. wurde die Umsetzung seiner Ideen fortgesetzt. Es wurde die von Bartolomeo Carlo Rastrelli geschaffene Gruppe von zwei auf dem Muschelhorn blasenden Tritonen aufgestellt. Die Kaskade schmückten zahlreiche Statuen, die nach Gipsformen der antiken Originalen gegossen wurden. Vor der Großen Grotte stellte man die Fontäne

# LE PARC INFÉRIEUR ET LE JARDIN SUPÉRIEUR

Une vue exceptionnelle sur le Parc Inférieur et la mer s'ouvre d'une terrasse devant la façade nordique du Grand Palais. Au centre la Grande Cascade étincelle de l'or des sculptures et de l'argent des jets d'eau. Cette construction centrale du système grandiose de fontaines exprime l'idée principale de l'ensemble de Peterhof: la glorification des victoires de la Russie dans la lutte pour l'accès à la mer Baltique.

Ce n'était pas par hasard que Pierre le Grand choisit ce lieu pour sa résidence de campagne. En explorant les buttes voisines il découvrit à 20 kilomètres de Peterhof quelques bassins alimentés par des sources. En 1721 on y installa un système hydraulique par lequel l'eau coulait par gravitation jusqu'à des bassins du Jardin Supérieur pour s'élancer après en jets de fontaines du Parc Inférieur.

Le dessein de la composition de la Grande Cascade appartenait à l'empereur. Sous Pierre le Grand une grotte, une balustrade, des premiers bas-reliefs et des mascarons furent construits. En Hollande on fit fondu douze figures allégoriques et des vases décoratifs. A la mort de Pierre Ier ses idées continuaient à se réaliser. B. F. Rastrelli érigea un groupe de deux tritons sonnants de coquilles. Des statues nombreuses moulées d'après des originaux antiques décorèrent la Cascade. A l'entrée de la grotte on voit la fontaine La Corbeille qui a 28 jets croisés en forme de cercle. Les cascades de marbre blanc à quatre marches sont enfoncées dans les pentes de la terrasse, cinq cascades de chaque côté.

Au centre du bassin devant la Grande Cascade on admire Samson - la fontaine la plus puissante de Peterhof. La décision de sa construction fut adoptée en 1734 quand on célébrait

lion's jaws (a lion is a symbol on the Swedish coat of arms) with mighty effort, and a twenty meter high water column rushes upward. Eight gilt dolphins give way to eight jets towards the feet of the hero.

There are vast flower beds with pan fountains on both sides of the fountain. They play an important compositional part in the fountain scene to support the huge water column of Samson and organize the territory before the Great Cascade.

The central reservoir and the sea are connected with a straight marine canal. In the time of Peter I the canal was navigable and small ships could sail to the reservoir from the Gulf of Finland. On both sides of the canal there are the oldest fountains of Peterhof, Adam and Eve, eight paths run from each of the fountains to form two octagonal stars.

Peter's idea was that there should be a fountain cascade before each palace in the Lower Park. The Chessboard Hill is one of them which is at the end of the avenue leading from the Monplaisir Palace to the terrace slope. The fountain was so-called because of the four vast inclined stairs with the ornament imitating a chessboard. The entrance to the Upper Grotto is guarded by three dragons. Powerful water streams spurt from their open mouths down the staircase. There are ten Italian marble statues of ancient gods along the sides of the cascade.

The lawn before the Chessboard Hill is decorated with two Roman Fountains. These are the most beautiful fountains of Peterhof and are very much like those before St Peter's in Rome.

The easten part of the Lower Park houses the Pyramid and the Sun Fountains of original and complicated design.

In 1717 while visiting Versailles, Peter I was struck by the fountain in the form

Korb auf: in einem flachen Bassin sprühen achtundzwanzig geneigte Wasserstrahlen, die sich miteinander verflechten und an einen Blumenkorb erinnern. In die natürliche Neigung der Terrasse wurden vierstufige Kaskaden aus weißem Marmor eingebracht. Inmitten des weitläufigen Bassins der Großen Kaskade befindet sich die mächtigste Fontäne *Samson*. Der Entschluß über die Errichtung dieser Fontäne wurde im Jahre 1734 zu Ehren des 25 jährigen Sieges bei Poltawa gefaßt. Der aus Bronze gegossene Recke Samson reißt mit mächtiger Kraft dem Löwen den Rachen auf, aus dem ein 30 Meter hoher Wasserstrahl emporschießt (im Wappen von Schweden gibt es einen Löwen). Zu Füßen des Helden liegen acht vergoldete wasserspeiende Delphine.

Rechts und links von der Großen Kaskade erstrecken sich weitläufige Blumenparterres mit Schalen-Fontänen. Die Schalen-Fontänen spielen eine wichtige Rolle innerhalb der Wasserspiele im Mittelteil des Unteren Parks. Sie betonen gestalterisch die gewaltige Fontäne der Samsongruppe und organisieren den Raum des Parterres mit dem Großen Blumengarten.

Der pfeilgerade *Große- oder Samson-Kanal* führt von dem zentralen Bassin zum Meer. Zu Lebzeiten Peters I. war er schiffbar und kleine Schiffe liefen in ihn aus dem Finnischen Meerbusen ein. Zu beiden Seiten des Kanals stehen die zwei ältesten Fontänen Peterhofs - *Adam* und *Eva* - von denen acht Alleen strahlenförmig ausgehen.

Nach den Vorstellungen Peters I. sollte jedem Schloß im Unteren Park eine Fontänen-Kaskade entsprechen. So befindet sich am Ende der Allee, die vom Schloß Monplaisir zum Anhang der Terrasse führt, die Kaskade der *Schachbrettberg*. Die vier geneigten Stufen dieser Kaskade sind mit schwarzen und weißen Quadraten bemalt, daher stammt die Bezeichnung. Drei Drachen bewachen den Eingang in die Obere Grotte. Aus ihrem weitaufgerissenen Rachen schießen mächtige Wasserstrahlen, die auf den Stufen abwärts strömen. An den Seiten der

le vingtcinquème anniversaire de la victoire de l'armée russe sur les Suédois à la bataille de Poltava. Moulé en bronze un héros géant déchire d'un puissant effort la gueule du lion (dans les armoiries de Suède il y a un lion) d'où se précipite une colonne d'eau à la hauteur de 30 mètres. Huit dauphins d'or élancent des jets d'eau aux pieds du héros.

Des vastes parterres de fleurs avec des Fontaine-coupes à droite et à gauche jouent un rôle important à la décoration de la partie centrale du Parc Inférieur. Ils soutiennent une énorme colonne d'eau de Samson et organisent l'espace de parterre devant la Grande Cascade.

Un canal droit comme une flèche s'étend du bassin central à la mer. A l'époque de Pierre le Grand ce canal était navigable et des petits navires pouvaient entrer du côté du golfe. A ses côtés au fond du parc on trouve les plus vieilles fontaines de Peterhof, Adam et Eve. Des allées divergeant de ces fontaines forment deux étoiles à huit branches.

Selon le dessein de Pierre le Grand chaque palais du Parc Inférieur doit avoir sa cascade de fontaines. La Montagne de l'Echiquier se tient au bout d'une allée qui se prolonge de Monplaisir jusqu'à une pente de la terrasse. Quatre marches immenses sont peintes comme l'échiquier, ce que est à l'origine de son nom moderne. L'entrée à la grotte supérieur est gardée par trois dragons. Des flots d'eau puissants se jetent de leurs gueules ouvertes et tombent sur les marches. Dix statues de dieux antiques de marbre achetées en Italie ornent deux côtés de la Cascade. Deux Fontaines Romaines construites d'après le projet de B. F. Rastrelli décorent le parterre de la Montagne de l'Echiquier.

of a triumphal structure and instructed Michetti to make a replica. There are 505 jets in the fountain and the pyramid effect is gained thanks to the system of taps and variations in the dia meter of holes in the bronze board of the foundation that allows the water jets of seven hights to be maintained. The Sun Fountain was built in the middle of a large pond with four gilt dolphin figures in its corners shooting water jets out of their mouths. The central jet of the fountain is housed within a rotation lead column mounted on a water wheel. There are three gilt disks on the top of the column having 187 outlets for water jets that produce the impression of the sun's rays. When the Château de Marly was being built in the western section of the Lower Park, Michetti was ordered to design one more cascade which was called the Golden Hill Cascade. The architect's design followed all the instructions of the Emperor. They were wide stairs of white marble, figures of mythological gods, stone stairs with balustrades, copper plates under the stairs to produce an additional light effect through the prism of the falling sprays and the huge water columns at the foot of the staircase that made cascade extremely impressive. Peter I was interested not only in the hydraulic structures of the park but also in its planning. There are papers with his instructions as to the layout of the paths, the tree species to plant and the drainage system to be built. The Venus Garden near the Château de Marly and the Monplaisir Garden with the famous Frick and Wheatsheaf Fountains were made under his immediate guidance. The Upper Garden was first designed to solve domestic and technical problems. It was used as a kitchen garden and the three fountain reservoirs served as fish ponds. It

Kaskade stehen zehn Marmorplastiken mythologischen Inhalts, die aus Italien stammen. Im Parterre-Garten vor dem Schachbrettberg erheben sich zwei *Römische Fontänen*. Stilistisch ähneln sie sich den Fontänen vor der Peter-Kathedrale in Rom und gehören zu den schönsten in Peterhof. Im östlichen Teil des Unteren Parks befinden sich zwei einzigartige hydrotechnisch komplizierte Fontänen - *Pyramide* und *Sonne*. Im Jahre 1717 war Peter I. während seines Besuches in Frankreich neben anderen Neuigkeiten, die ihn in Versailles begeisterten, vor allem ein Springbrunnen aufgefallen, der die Form eines Obelisken hatte. Er beauftragte Michetti, diesen Springbrunnen nachzugestalten. Die Fontäne besteht aus 505 Kupferröhren, je nach ihrer Annäherung zum Zentrum des Springbrunnens verengt sich auch ihr Durchmesser und das Wasser schießt unter verschiedenem Druck in verschiedene Höhe empor, dadurch entsteht ein Pyramideneffekt. Die zweite Fontäne *Sonne* wurde in der Mitte des geräumigen Bassins errichtet. Im Sockel der hohen Stange ist ein Wasserrad untergebracht, so daß die Stange rotiert. Ganz oben an der Stange sind parallel zueinander angeordnete Scheiben befestigt. Diese vergoldeten Scheiben haben 187 Öffnungen. Die aus ihnen herausschießenden Wasserstrahlen erinnern an Sonnen-strahlen. Im Jahre 1720, als mit dem Bau des Schlosses *Marly* begonnen wurde, beauftragte Peter I. Niccolo Michetti mit dem Entwurf einer weiteren Kaskade, die als *Goldener Berg* bezeichnet wurde. Der Architekt entwarf die Kaskade ganz nach Peters Wunsch. Breite Stufen aus weißem Marmor, Statuen antiker Götter, steinerne Treppen mit Balustraden und vergoldete Kupferplatten an den Stufen erzeugen ein einmaliges Lichtspiel im Spiegel des herunterströmenden Wassers. Die mächtigen Wasserstrahlen, die am Ende der Wassertreppe in die Luft scheinen, lassen die Marly-Kaskade besonders effektvoll wirken. Peter I. interessierte sich nicht nur für hydrotechnische Bauten, sondern widmete sein Interesse auch der

Peut-être sont-elles les plus belles fontaines de Peterhof et elles ressemblent beaucoup à celles de la place devant la Cathédral de St.-Pierre à Rome. La Pyramide et Le Soleil - ces deux fontaines originales et compliquées sont à la partie d'Est du Parc Inférieur. Quand Pierre le Grand fut en France en 1717 parmi les beautés de Versailles il prêta attention à une fontaine qui se dressait comme une construction triomphale et proposa à Michetti de faire la même. On arrive à l'effet de pyramide avec les 505 tubes dont les diamètres dégressifs donnent l'augmentation de pression d'eau. L'autre fontaine - Le Soleil - se trouve au milieu d'un vaste bassin qui servait autrefois pour les baignades. Au sommet d'une colonne qui se tourne avec une roue à eau on attacha 3 disques parallèles avec 187 orifices. Les disques tournoyant, des jets d'eau passent par les orifices et ressemblent aux rayons divergents du soleil. Quand on commença à ériger le Palais de Marly Pierre le Grand chargea Michetti de faire le plan d'une cascade qu'on nomma La Montage d'or. L'architecte élabora le plan en conformité des désirs de l'empereur. Des larges marches de marbre blanc descendent de la hauteur de 14 mètres, des sculptures de dieux antiques, des escaliers de pierre avec balustrades, des feuilles dorées sous les marches font un jeu original de la lumière à travers l'eau. Et enfin des jets d'eau gigantésques s'élancent vers le ciel au bas de l'escalier. Tout cela donne une vue extraordinaire à cette Cascade. Il faut dire que Pierre le Grand s'intéressait non seulement aux constructions hydrauliques mais aussi à la planification du Parc. Il y a des documents qui nous sont parvenus où on trouve ses instructions sur le tracé des

was not until the second half of the 18th century that the kitchen garden was turned into a regular French garden. The main element of its decoration is the ensemble of the Neptune Fountain cast in Nuremberg. The main part of the Upper Garden was to be the gala entrance to the Great Palace.

Parkgestaltung.
Entsprechend seiner Anweisungen entstanden Alleen, wurden Bestimmte Baumarten angepflanzt und das Dränage-System angelegt. Unter Peters persönlicher Anweisung entstanden der *Venus*-Garten in der Nähe von Marly, sowie der *Monplaisir-Parterre*-Garten mit der Fontäne Garbe und den berühmten *Scherzfontänen*.
Der Obere Garten diente als Gemüsegarten: auf Beeten wurde Gemüse angepflanzt, die drei größen Teiche, die das Fontänensystem speisten, benutzte man zur Fischzucht. In der zweiten Hälfte des 18 Jahrhunderts wurde dieser Gemüsegarten in einen französischen Garten umgestaltet.
Der Hauptschmuck dieses Gartens ist die in Nürnberg gegossene Skulpturgruppe der Fontäne *Neptun* Heutzutage dient der Obere Garten als Paradehof des Großen Schlosses.

allées, sur les espèces d'arbres à planter, sur le système de drainage. Sous sa diréction immédiate on traça le Jardin de Vénus près de Marly et le Jardin de Monplaisir avec la fontaine La Gerbe et les célèbres Fontaines à surprise.
Quant au Jardin Supérieur, celuici jouait avant tout un rôle économique. On y plantait des légumes et alevinait des poissons dans trois étangs qui servaient de réservoirs d'eau pour les fontaines. Ce n'est qu'à la seconde moitié du XVIIIme s. que ce Potager (comme l'on nommait) prit l'image d'un jardin régulier à la française. Sa décoration principalle est le groupe des sculptures de la fontaine Neptune moulées à Nuremberg. En gros, le Jardin Supérieur joue le rôle de cour d'honneur principale du Grand Palais.

17. Great Cascade. Samson Fountain.
Große Kaskade. Fontäne Samson.
La Grande Cascade. La fontaine Samson.

**19.** Great Cascade. Basket Fountain.

Große Kaskade. Fontäne *Korb*.

La Grande Cascade. La fontaine *Corbeille*.

▷

**20.** Great Cascade. General View.

Große Kaskade. Gesamtansicht.

La Grande Cascade. Vue générale.

**18.** Western Cascade Staircase. *Ganymede*. Copy of the Antique original.

Westliche Kaskade-Treppe. *Ganymed*. Kopie nach einem antiken Original.

L'escalier d'ouest de la Cascade. *Ganymède* - copie d'original antique.

**21.** Bigger or *Bowl* Fountain.
Architect N.Michetti, 1721-1725,
A.Stakenschneider, 1854.

Große Fontäne oder Fontäne *Schale.*
Architekten N.Michetti, 1721-1725,
A.Stakenschneider, 1854.

Grande Fontaine, ou Fontaine-*coupe.*
Architectes N.Michetti. 1721-1725,
A.Stakenschneider. 1854.

**22.** *Adam* Fountain.
Sculptor G.Bonazza, 1718.
Architect N.Michetti, 1722.

Fontäne *Adam.*
Bildhauer G.Bonazza, 1718.
Architekt N.Michetti, 1722.

Fontaine *Adam.*
Sculpteur G.Bonazza, 1718.
Architecte N.Michetti, 1722.

**23.** *Eve* Fountain.
Sculptor G.Bonazza, 1718.
Architects N.Michetti, T.Usov, 1726.

Fontäne *Eva.*
Bildhauer G.Bonazza, 1718.
Architekten N.Michetti, T.Usow, 1726.

Fontaine *Eve.*
Sculpteur G.Bonazza, 1718.
Architectes N.Michetti, T.Oussov, 1726.

▷
**24.** *Chessboard Hill* Cascade.
Architects M.Zemtsov, I.Blank,
I.Davydov, 1737-1739.

*Schachbrettberg*-Kaskade.
Architekten M.Semzow, I.Blank,
I.Dawydow, 1737-1739.

Cascade *La Montagne de l'Echiquier.*
Architectes M.Zemtsov, I.Blanc,
I.Davidov, 1737-1739.

**25.** *Sun* Fountain.
Architects N.Michetti, 1724, J.Velten,
I.Yakovlev, 1772-1776.

Fontäne *Sonne.*
Architekten N.Michetti, 1724, J.Velten,
I.Jakowlew, 1772-1776.

Fontaine *Le Soleil.*
Architectes N.Michetti. 1724, J.Felten,
I.Iakovlev, 1772-1776.

**26.** *Triton* Bell-Fountain.
Architect I.Braunstein, 1721.

Glocken-Fontäne *Triton.*
Architekt I.Braunstein, 1721.

Fontaine-Cloche *Triton.*
Architecte I.Braunstein, 1721.

**27.** *Roman* Fountain.
Architects I.Blank, I. Davydov, 1738-
1739, B.F.Rastrelli, 1763.

*Römische* Fontäne.
Architekten I.Blank, I.Dawydow, 1738-
1739, B.F.Rastrelli, 1763.

Fontaine *Romaine.*
Architectes I.Blanc, I.Davidov, 1738-
1739, B.F.Rastrelli, 1763.

**28.** *Neptune* Fountain. 1799.
Sculptural group by Ch.Ritter
and G.Schweigger, 1650-1660.

Fontäne *Neptun*. 1799.
Skulpturgruppe von Ch.Ritter,
und G.Schweigger, 1650-1660
ausgeführt.

Fontaine *Neptune.* 1799.
Groupe sculpté, par Ch.Ritter,
G.Schweigger, 1650-1660.

# CHÂTEAU DE MARLY

The Château de Marly is situated in the western part of the Lower Park. It was built by the architect Johann-Friedrich Braunstein in 1720-1727. The name was derived from the residence of French kings in Marly-de-Roi near Paris. This small two-storey building is of great importance to the park layout. It marks the start of the three main ray-like avenues - the Central Marly, the North Maliban and the South Birch Tree Avenues.

Construction work was begun here with the creation of rectangular and semicircular basins. These artificial reservoirs, besides esthetic needs, met domestic ones and were used as fish ponds.

There are 14 rooms in the palace. On the ground floor there are the Kitchen and the Pantry where brass and tin kitchen- and table-ware of the 17-18th centuries are displayed. The glass flasks and bottles with the words "Danzig" and "London" that belonged to Peter I are of particular interest. There are some more personal things of the Emperor in the Bedroom - his blanket, towel and a set of porcelain vases.

The largest room on the ground floor is the Front Hall designed as the official vestibule. There are two canvases on its walls - *Christ Preaching in the Temple* by Tiziano Vecellio, Tizian's descendant, and *Christ and the Adulteress* by Andrea Celesti. The present collection of 45 paintings of European artists used to decorate the palace in the time of Peter I.

The staircase leading to the first floor brings one to the door of the Wardrobe Room. Once the Château de Marly was the main depository of the Emperor's clothing. Then a greater part of it was moved to the Hermitage in St Petersburg. But even the few objects presented here are regarded as precious relics of Peter's age.

# SCHLOß MARLY

Beinahe an der Westgrenze des Unteren Parks befindet sich noch ein Schloß aus der Zeit Peters I. - das Schloß *Marly*. Das Schloß wurde von 1720 bis 1725 von dem Architekten Johann-Friedrich Braunstein errichtet. Seine Bezeichnung geht auf die französische Königsresidenz in Marly-de-Roi bei Paris zurück. Ungeachtet seiner bescheidener Größe spielt dieser zweigeschossige Bau eine bedeutende Rolle in der Gesamtgestaltung des Unteren Parks. Von ihm gehen strahlenförmig drei Alleen aus: in der Mitte die *Marly-Allee*, nach Norden hin die *Maliban-Allee* und nach Süden hin die *Birken-Allee*. Das Schloß liegt zwischen dem großen rechteckigen Teich und dem kleineren halbkreisförmigen Teich. Die Bauarbeiten begannen mit der Anlage dieser Teiche, in denen ursprünglich Fische gezüchtet wurden. Die ausgenommene Erde wurde zur Errichtung eines großen Damms genutzt. Dieser Damm sollte vor Überschwemmungen und andererseits vor dem nördlichen Wind schützen.

Im Schloß gibt es 14 Räume. In der ersten Etage befinden sich die *Küche* und das *Anrichtezimmer*, in denen Geschirr aus Kupfer und Zinn sowie Tafelgeschirr aus dem 17.-18. Jahrhundert ausgestellt sind. Von besonderem Interesse sind die Glasstoffe mit der Inschrift "Danzig" und "London".

Im *Schlafzimmer* sind eine Bettdecke, ein Handtuch und Fayence-Vasen, die Peter I. gehörten, zu sehen.

Der größte Raum in der ersten Etage ist der *Vordere Saal* in der Funktion eines Vestibüls. Seine Wände sind mit den Gemälden *Christus predigt im Gottes-haus* von Andrea Celesti und *Christus und die Sünderin* von

# PALAIS DE MARLY

A l'ouest en sens contraire de Monplaisir se dresse un palais de l'époque de Pierre le Grand érigé en 1720-1723 par J.-F. Braunstein. C'est la résidence des rois français Marly-de-Roi près de Paris qui donna le nom au Palais.

Ce petit édifice à un étage joue un rôle important à l'agencement du Parc Inférieur. Les trois allées principales rayonnent d'ici: celle de Marly au milieu, celle de Maliban au nord et celle des Bouleaux au sud.

Les travaux commencèrent par la construction de deux étangs: rectangle et semi-circulaire. Ces bassins furent faits non seulement pour les buts esthétiques, mais aussi économiques - on y élevait des poissons. Le sol pris des bassins servit pour une grande digue. Un rempart en terre défendait le Palais d'inondation et de vent du nord.

Le palais comporte 14 pièces. La cuisine du style hollandais et l'Office sont au rez-de-chaussée. C'est ici que sont réunis la batterie de cuisine d'étain et de cuivre, les services de table des XVIIme-XVIIIme ss. Les objets qui ayant appartenu à Pierre Ier présentent l'intérèt particulier: les gourdes et les bouteilles en verre aux inscriptions "Dantsig" et "Londres", sa couverture, la serviette et la garniture de vases de faïence.

Grande salle, la plus vaste pièce du rez-de-chaussée sert du vestibule d'honneur. Ses murs sont ornés de toiles *Le Christ préchant au Temple*" de A.Celesti et *Le Christ et la femme adultère* de Titien Vecellio (un descen-dant du grand Titien). La collection qui compte aujourd'hui des 45 tableaux de peintres européens fit partie du décor de Palais à l'époque de Pierre. Monté au premier étage on se trouve devant la Garde-robe. C'est au palais

A considerable part of the Sitting Room on the first floor is occupied by a cabinet with ebony and turtle decorations, made in Augsburg, Bavaria. The centre of the Dining Room is given to a large table of the 16th century of English craftwork. The chairs running along the walls were made in Flandria. The doors lead from the Dining Room to the Library and to the Study.

There were libraries in all the palaces of Peter I as a rule. The books of the Château de Marly as well as the displayed English globe and the picture *The Port and the Town Gate of Rotterdam* - by A. Stork can give a notion of the taste of their owner. The comfort of the small Oak Study was very conducive to work and thought, and the open book on the Italian marquetry cabinet proves this. The desk with a slate bourd near the window, as the legend says, was made by the Emperor himself. There is a universal sun-dial on the desk.

Tizian Vecellio, einem Großneffen von dem großen Tizian. Die heutige Sammlung in Marly umfaßt 45 Arbeiten westeuropäischer Maler, die meisten befanden sich schon zu Zeiten Peters I. im Schloß. Am oberen Ende der Treppe liegt das *Ankleidezimmer*. Das Schloß *Marly* war ursprünglich der Hauptaufbewahrungsort der Garderobe Peters I.. Später wurde der größte Teil davon der Kaiserlichen Ermitage in Petersburg übergeben. Doch auch die im Schloß verbliebenen Gegenstände: ein Seemannmantel und Kaftan mit aufgesticktem Emblem des Andreas-Ordens sind wertvolle Reliquien aus der petrinischen Zeit. Einen großen Teil des *Gastzimmers* in der zweiten Etage nimmt das mit schwarzem Holz und Schildpatt verzierte *Kabinett* ein. Es wurde in Bayern, in Augsburg, angefertigt. Im *Speisezimmer* steht ein großer Tisch, eine englische Arbeit aus dem 16. Jahrhundert. Die Stühle an der Wand stammen aus Flandern. Die Türen aus dem *Speisezimmer* führen in die *Bibliothek* und in das *Kabinett*.

Sogar in den kleinen Schlössern Peters I. gab es immer Bücher. In der Bibliothek in Marly befinden sich ein englischer Globus und das Gamälde *'Hafen mit dem Stadttor in Amsterdam'* von A.Stork. Beides läßt auf den Geschmack ihres Besitzers schließen.

Das gemütliche kleine *Eichholzkabinett* diente als Arbeits- und Denkplatz. Daran erinnern die aufgeschlagenen Bücher auf dem Sekretär, einer italienischen Arbeit. Am Fenster steht ein Tisch mit einer Schieferplatte, der soll von Peter I. angefertigt worden sein. Auf dem Tisch steht eine universale Sonnenuhr.

de Marly qu'auparavant on gardait les effets de Pierre le Grand. Quelque temps après la plupart des affaires fut remise à l'Ermitage à Saint-Pétersbourg. Mais son manteau de marin et son habit à une broderie représentant l'ordre d'Apôtre André qui sont restés ici sont des réliques précieuses de l'époque petrovienne.

Une grande partie de Salon du premier étage est occupée par le bureau orné d'ébène et d'écaille. Il fut réalisé en Bavière, à Ausbourg. A la Salle à manger se trouve une grande table anglaise du XVIme s. Les fauteuils s'allongeant contre les murs furent fait en Flandres. Les portes de la Salle à manger donnent sur la Bibliothèque et le Cabinet de chêne.

On trouve les livres dans tous les palais de Pierre le Grand, même dans ses petites résidences. La Bibliothèque de Marly avec un globe anglais et un tableau de A.Stork *Le port et les portes de Rotterdam* représentent les goûts de son hôte.

L'atmosphère de confort du petit Cabinet de chêne favorisait le travail et les méditations. Des livres ouverts exposés sur le bureau en marqueterie italien en parlent avec éloquence. Près de la fenêtre sur une table exécutée par Pierre le Grand, comme on le prétend, on voit un cadran solaire.

**29.** Château de Marly Palace.
View from the *Golden Hill* Cascade.

Schloß Marly.
Blick von der Kaskade *Goldener Berg*.

Palais de Marly.
Vue de la Cascade *La Montagne d'or*.

**30.** Entrance Hall.

Vorderer Saal.

Grand Salle.

**31.** Fragment of the Entrance Hall.
Clock. W.Coster. Holland.
Mid 18th century.

Vorderer Saal. Teilansicht.
Standuhr. W.Coster. Holland.
Mitte des 18. Jahrhunderts.

Grand Salle. Détail.
Pendule. W.Coster. Hollande.
Milieu du XVIIIe s.

**32.** Kitchen.
Küche.
Cuisine.

**33.** Cooking utensils of Russian and West European craftwork of the 18th century.

Küchengeschir russischer und westeuropäischen Arbeit aus dem 18. Jahrhundert.

Batterie de cuisine. Russie, Europe occidentale. XVIIe s.

**34.** Dining Hall.
Speisesaal.
Salle à manger.

**35.** Oak Study.
Eichenholzkabinett.
Cabinet de chêne.

**36.** Library. Globe.
England. First half of the 18th century.

Bibliothek. Globus.
England. Erste Hälfte des 18.
Jahrhunderts.

Bibliothèque. Globe.
Angleterre. Première moitié du XVIIIe s.

**37.** View from the Oak Study.

Blick aus dem Fenster des
Eichenholzkabinetts.

Vue du Cabinet de chêne.

# HERMITAGE PAVILION

In the heart of the Lower Park, on the sea-shore, stands an elegant two-storey building - the first Hermitage in Russia (1721-1725, architect J.- F.Braunstein). Above the entrance is a balcony with wrought-iron railings. The high French windows, through which the light flows inside freely, give the building a special airiness. The building is surrounded by a deep moat. Only a drawbridge links it with the outside world.

Peter the Great got the idea to build the Hermitage during his visit to Europe where this type of pavilion was in fashion. But the Emperor was not destined to see the Hermitage built because its construction was completed only in the summer of 1725, after his death.

On the ground floor are the Pantry and the Kitchen where the dishes were warmed prior to serving. In the 18th century one could reach the first floor only by the lift-chair for two persons, operated by the windlass. This lift worked right up until the end of the 18th century. In 1797, when Emperor Paul I and his family were going up in the lift-chair, the mechanism jammed and the noble passengers were rescued with the help of a ladder. Orders were given for the mechanism to be removed and the present stairs to be built.

The whole of the first floor is taken up by one very light and airy room, the reason why the building was erected. The room was intended as a place to retire with an intimate circle of friends. Fourteen persons could sit at the large oval table in the centre of the room. Each had a place set for him, and the central part of the table with the requisite cutlery, dishes, ets. was hauled up from the Pantry through a special chute. Yet each of the guests could order a dish just for himself. All he was to do was to write down his request on a piece of paper, put it on a plate and pull a cord. A bell

# PAVILLON ERMITAGE

Im westlichen Teil des Unteren Gartens steht an der Küste des Meeres ein elegantes zweigeschos-siges Gebäude. Das war Rußlands erste *Ermitage*. Die wurde in den Jah-ren 1721 bis 1725 von dem Architekten Johann -Friedrich Braunstein errichtet. Der Balkon über dem Ein-gang überrascht durch sein Metallgitter mit bizarrem Muster in präziser Ausführung. Hohe Fenster und verglaste Türen, die den Blick in das Innere freigeben, verleihen dem Bau eine besondere Leichtigkeit. Um das Gebäude herum zieht sich ein tiefer Graben, der mit Ziegelsteinen ausgelegt und mit Wasser gefüllt ist. Eine kleine Brücke verbindet den Pavillon mit dem Festland. Peter I. beschloß die *Ermitage* zu bauen, nachdem er von einer Reise durch Europa zurückgekehrt war, wo Pavillons dieser Art Mode waren. Es war ihm aber nicht gewahrt, diesen Pavillon vollendet zu sehen – die Bauarbeiten wurden im Sommer 1725, nach Peters Tod erst abgeschlossen.

Im Erdgeschoß befinden sich die *Küche* und das *Anrichtezimmer*. Im 18. Jahrhundert konnte man nur mit Hilfe eines heraufziehbaren Ses-sels für zwei Personen in die obere Etage gelangen. Dieser "Fahrstuhl" funktionierte bis 1797. Während des Aufenthaltes Pauls I. und seiner Familie fiel das Antriebssystem aus. Der "Fahrstuhl" blieb zwischen den Geschossen stecken. Der Zar befahl daraufhin die Hebevorrichtung abzumontieren und eine neue Treppe zu bauen, die bis heute existiert. Das gesamte Obereschoß besteht aus einem einzigen Raum voller Licht und Luft. Gerade seinetwegen wurde der Pavillon errichtet; Hier kamen die Zarenfamilie und ihre nächsten Freunde für kurzweiligen Zeitvertrieb zusammen. Vierzehn Personen fanden an dem großen ovalen

# L'ERMITAGE

Au fond du Parc Inférieur au bord de la mer s'élève un élégant bâtiment à un étage. C'est le premier Ermitage russe, erigé en 1721-1725 par J.-F.Braunstein. Au-dessus de son entrée se trouve le balcon à une grille en ferronnerie ouvragée avec beaucoup d'art. De grandes portes-fenêtres à travers lesquelles passe la lumière donnent la légèreté singulière au Pavillon. L'édifice est entouré d'un fossé profond et un petit pont le relie à la terre.

Pierre eut l'idée de construire l'Ermitage pendant son voyage en Europe où des pavillons pareils étaient à la mode. Mais il ne vit pas son projet achevé. Les travaux ne se finirent qu'après sa mort, en été 1725.

Au rez-de-chaussée se trouvent la Cuisine et l'Office où on réchauffait des plats pour servir la table. Au XVIIIme s. on ne pouvait pénétrer à l'étage qu'avec le fauteuil mécanique de levage pour deux personnes. Cet ascenseur fonctionna sans pannes jusqu'à 1797 quand l'empereur Paul Ier visita l'Ermitage. Soudain le mécanisme se coinça et il fallait évacuer les augustes personnes par une échelle. On ordonna aussitôt de détruire le mécanisme et de construire l'escalier qui existe toujours.

Le premier étage est occupé par une seule vaste salle pleine de lumière et d'air, et c'est la raison d'être de ce pavillon. C'est ici que se rassemblait un petit cercle des amis les plus proches de l'hôte. Quatorze personnes prennaient places autour de la table ovale au centre. Chacun avait un couvert devant soi. La partie centrale de la table avec tout le service et des plats était montée du rez-de-chaussée par un puits spécial. Pourtant les convives pouvaient commander un plat à leur goût. Alors il fallait noter une

then rang downstairs in the Pantry, and the servants lowered the plate down a chute. Then the plate was sent up with the order.

The hall's main decorations, which make it look magnificent and festive, are 124 pictures by West European artists bought on the order of Peter the Great. Among them are battle scenes by the highly popular 17th-century painter Jacques Courtois, still lifes by another Frenchman Jean Louis Prevost, seascapes by two Dutch painters and paintings of the Apostles by the Dutch painter Georg Gsell, favoured by Peter I. Other works of interest are Giovanni Battista Lan getti's *Death of Cato*, depicting the suicide of this tribune of the people in Ancient Rome who refused to submit to the dictatorship of Caesar; paintings by two other Italians - Giulio Carpioni and Gaspare Diziani. The collection contains a copy of a large painting *The Battle of Poltava*, commissioned by Peter I from Pierre Martin. The copy is the work of an unknown Russian artist.

The small but rich and varied collection of the Hermitage in Peterhof enables us to form an idea of the way paintings were collected in 18th-century Russia.

Tisch Platz. Vor jedem stand ein Gedeck. Der mittlere Teil der Tischplatte wurde durch eine spezielle Öffnung mit Hilfe von zwei Winden in das Anrichtezimmer herabgelassen. War die Tafel vollständig serviert, wurde sie nach oben gezogen. Trotzdem konnte jeder der Gäste auch noch individuell Speisen bestellen. Dazu mußte der entsprechende Wunsch auf einen Zettel geschrieben und auf den Teller gelegt werden. Dann zog man an einer Schnur. In dem Anrichtezimmer läutete ein Glöckchen. Ein Diener ließ den Teller nach unten, und kurze Zeit darauf erschien das bestellte Gericht vor dem Gast.

Den Hauptschmuck des Saales bilden die hundertvierundzwanzig Gemälde westeuropäischer Meister, die dem Saal ein besonders festliches Aussehen verleihen. Die Gemälde wurden im Auftrag Peters I. erworben. Das sind Werke des populärsten Schlachtenmalers aus dem 17. Jahrhundert, Jacques Courtois und Stilleben des Franzosen Jean Lois Prevost, Seestücke holländischer Maler und Darstellungen der Apostel vom holländischen Maler Georg Gsell, der von Peter I. besonders geschätzt wurde. An der gleichen Wand hängt das Gemälde *Tod Catos* von Giovanni Battista Langetti: das Thema des Gemäldes ist der Selbstmord des Volkstribuns des Alten Roms der sich der Diktatur Cäsars nicht unterwerfen wollte. In der Sammlung gibt es auch Arbeiten der Italiener Giulio Carpioni und Caspare Diziani. An einer Wand hängt das Gemälde *Schlacht bei Poltawa* eines unbekannten russischen alers. Die kleine, in ihrer usammensetzung und Mannigfaltigkeit der Werke aber hervorragende Kollektion der Peterhofer Ermitage ermöglicht es, sich eine Vorstellung über die Sammlungen von Werken der bildenden Kunst in Rußland im 18. Jahrhundert zu verschaffen.

commande sur un billet, le placer sur une assiette et tirer un cordonnet. Une clochette sonnait à l'Office, un serviteur faisait descendre l'assiette et ensuite la faisait remonter garnie du plat commandé.

Mais la décoration principale de la Salle qui lui donne de la solennité et de l'apparat c'est la collection des 124 tableaux de peintres européens achetés sur la commande de Pierre le Grand - des toiles du célèbre peintre de bataille J. Courtois et des natures mortes de J.-L. Prévost, des marines des Hollandais, Apôtres de G .Gsell, favorit de Pierre le Grand. On y admire *La mort de Caton* de G. B. Langetti qui représente le suicide du tribun réfusant d'obeir à la dictature de César; des œuvres de G. Carpioni et G. Diziani. On y voit aussi un grand tableau *La Bataille de Poltava*. C'est une copie executée par le peintre français P. D. Martin sur l'ordre de Pierre Ier. La collection de l'Ermitage pas grande mais remarquable par son contenu et sa diversité permet de se faire une idée de l'esprit de collectionnement de la peinture au XVIIIme s. en Russie.

38. Hermitage Pavilion.
Pavillon Ermitage.
Pavillon de L'Hermitage.

**39.** Dining Hall.

Speisesaal.

Salle à manger.

40. *The Battle of Poltava.*
Copy by P.Martin from the painting
of an unknown artist.

*Die Schlacht bei Poltawa.*
Kopie von P.Martin nach dem Gemälde
eines unbekannten Malers.

*La Bataille de Poltava.*
Copie par P.D.Martin de l'original
de peintre anonyme.

**41.** Fragment of the Dining Hall.

Speisesaal. Teilansicht.

Salle à manger. Détail.

# MONPLAISIR

There is an artificial terrace strengthened with huge granite boulders projecting out to the sea. A one-storey brick building behind it is the Monplaisir Palace, the favourite of Peter I. The site for the construction was chosen and the plan of the palace was worked out by the Emperor himself. However far away he was, even abroad, he used to send instructions concerning the decoration of the Monplaisir interiors. The building of the palace was performed by the architects J.-F.Braunstein, J.-B.Le Blond and N.Michetti.

There are two galleries next to each side of the palace hung with pictures of West European masters of the 17th and the beginning of the 18th centuries. Peter I liked sea-scapes particularly, which is why Dutch and Flemish painters are the most numerous here, their works being bought at auctions in Amsterdam.

Adjacent to the East Gallery is the Lacquered Study, its walls are decorated with black lacquered panels with landscapes in oriental style. The central room of the palace is the Ceremonial Hall. The official character of the room designed for gala receptions is emphasized by its large dimensions and the rich décor. The walls are covered with oak panels and paintings mounted in them are pictures of ships at sea by Adam Silo. Peter I is said to have used them to examine students of the Russian Naval Academy.

But the most remarkable feature of the Hall is its four-facet dome-shaped ceiling painted by the French master Philippe Pillement.

Mythological gods symbolizing the four nature elements - Water, Air, Fire and Earth are painted on each side. The pair of sculptures in the corners symbolize the four seasons, and Apollo, the god of poetry, art and the sun,

# SCHLOß MONPLAISIR

Im östlichen Teil des Unteren Parks ragt eine künstliche Terrasse ins Meer, die mit Granitblöcken befestigt ist. An ihrem Rand entlang zieht sich eine weiße Balustrade, hinter der man ein eingeschossiges Backsteingebäude mit abgestuftem Terrassendach sieht. Das ist das Lustschlößchen *Monplaisir*, die Lieblingsresidenz Peters I.. Peter I. selbst wählte den Platz für dieses Schloß aus und erarbeitete den Bauplan. Wo sich der Zar auch aufhielt, selbst aus dem Ausland schickte er Anweisungen, wie das Interieur des Schlosses zu gestalten sei.

Vom Zentralbau aus verlaufen zwei durchgehende Galerien, in denen Gemälde der europäischen Künstler aus dem 17. und 18. Jahrhundert ausgestellt sind. Peter I. bevorzugte Seestücke, darum sind hier hauptsächlich Arbeiten holländischer und flämischer Maler ausgestellt, die man auf Auktionen in Amsterdam erworben hatte.

Aus der Östlichen Galerie gelangt man in das *Lackkabinett*. Große schwarzlackierte Panneaus mit orientalischen Landschaften sind die Hauptattraktion dieses Raumes. Neben diesem Kabinett liegt der *Paradesaal*. Der Charakter des Raumes, der für festliche Empfänge bestimmt war, wird durch seine Größe und seine prunkvolle Ausstattung betont. An den eichenholzgetäfelten Wänden hängen Gemälde, darunter fünf mit Darstellungen von Schiffen auf der Reede von Adam Silo. Man sagt, daß Peter I. die Schüler der russischen Marineakademie anhand von Silos Gemälden prüfte.

Von besonderem Interesse ist die Bemalung der kuppelartigen Überwölbung von Philippe Pillement. An den Vouten sind in Gestalt von vier antiken Göttern die vier Elemente: Wasser,

# LE PALAIS DE MONPLAISIR

A l'est du Parc Inférieur une haute terrasse artificielle renforcée de blocs de granit fait saillie à la mer. Derrière elle on voit un édifice de brique sans étages à la toiture élevée. C'est le Palais de Monpaisir, l'œuvre de prédilection de Pierre le Grand. L'empereur lui-même choisit l'emplacement du Palais et élabora son plan. Où qu'il fût, même à l'étranger, il envoyait des inscriptions relatives au garnissage des intérieurs de Monplaisir.

Deux Galeries qui contiennent des tableaux des peintres européens du XVIIe s. au XVIIIe s. confinent au Palais. Comme Pierre le Grand aimait surtout les marines, ce sont les peintres hollandais et flamands dont les œuvres furent acquis aux enchères d'Amsterdam qui dominent.

A la sortie de la Galerie Est on se trouve au Cabinet laqué dont les murs sont garnis de panneaux de laque noire aux sujets orientals. Ensuite on pénètre dans la Salle d'apparat où on donnait des réceptions. La grandeur et la richesse du décor soulignent son caractère d'apparat. Les murs sont ornés de tableaux dans des plaques carrés de chêne. C'est parmi ces tableaux qu'on voit 5 toiles de A.Silo représentant des navires en rade.

On prétend que Pierre le Grand se servait de ces tableaux aux examens des élèves de l'Ecole Navale.

La chose la plus remarquable dans cette salle est le plafond peint par Ph. Pillement. Aux voussures les quatre éléments (l'Eau, l'Air, le Feu, la Terre) sont représentés par des figures de dieux de l'Antiquité, aux coins - des allégories de quatre saisons, au centre - dieu des arts et du soleil Apollon.

A l'aide de ces symboles l'artiste parle des changements de monde, du retour

is in the centre above them all. The painter uses the language of symbols to illustrate the world's changeability, the seasonal rotation and transient time. Only art, he says, is eternal.

The next rooms on the west end of the Ceremonial Hall are the Kitchen decorated with tile brought from the Dutch town of Delft and the Pantry housing a rich collection of ceramic and glasswear. The eight tea pots on the fire-place were presented to Peter I by the Emperor of China.

The private apartments of Peter I - the Marine Study and the Bedroom are at the east end of the Hall. Kronstadt and St Petersburg can be seen through the study windows. Peter liked this room. He would watch the ships sailing about the Gulf of Finland using his telescope.

In the Bedroom the walls are covered with cloth and the bed has a heavy canopy as in other palaces of Peter I. One can see a dressing gown and a night cap on the bed as well as a Spanish table, a wooden mug, a jar and a tray made in England.

All these are the personal things of Peter I.

Later Rastrelli added service galleries and a large wing given the name of Catherine. Catherine II had lived in it, being in disgrace before she became the Empress in 1762.

Luft, Feuer und Erde dargestellt. An den Ecken sind paarige Skulpturgruppen, die die vier Jahrzeiten personifizieren. Und in der Mitte über ihnen allen herrscht der Sonnengott Apollo, der Beschützer der Künste. Mittels der Symbole berichtet der Künstler von der Unbeständigkeit der Welt, vom Kreislauf der Jahreszeiten und von der Vergänglichkeit der Zeit. Nur die Kunst ist ewig und unsterblich.

An den *Paradesaal* schließ sich an der Westseite die Küche an, die mit Kacheln aus der holländischen Stadt Delft verkleidet ist. Daneben ist das *Anrichtezimmer*. Auf den Regalen und dem Küchenschrank steht verschiedenes Geschirr aus Glas und Keramik. Auf dem Kamin sind acht Teekannen, die Peter I. von dem chinesischen Kaiser geschenkt bekommen hatte.

An der Ostseite des Paradesaales befinden sich Privaträume Peters I.: das *Schlafzimmer* und das *Marinekabinett*. Aus den Fenstern des Kabinetts kann man auf der einen Seite Kronstadt, auf der anderen Seite Petersburg sehen. Peter I. hielt sich gern in diesem Raum. Er öffnete die untere Hälfte des Fensters und beobachtete durch ein Fernrohr die Takelung der auf dem Finnischen Meerbusen vorbeikommenden Schiffe.

Die Wände des *Schlafzimmers* sind mit Stoff bespannt, über dem Bett liegen Peters Morgenrock und seine Schlafmütze. Im *Schlafzimmer* werden einige persönliche Gegenstände Peters I. aufbewahrt: ein mit Kupferplatten beschlagener Tisch, eine spanische Arbeit, ein hölzerner Becher, ein Waschkrug und ein Becken englischer Arbeit. Später baute Rastrelli erdgeschossige Dienstgebäude und ein Gebäude, das als *Katharina-Trakt* bezeichnet wurde. Dort mußte sich Katharina II. aufhalten, bevor sie im Jahre 1762 den Thron bestieg.

des saisons, de la fuite du temps. Selon lui, c'est l'art qui est éternel, immortel.

La porte du mur est de la Salle d'apparat mène à la Cuisine ornée de carreaux de faïences apportés de Delft et à l'Office où une riche collection de vaisselle de céramique et de verrerie est exposée.

Les appartements privés de l'empereur: la Chambre à coucher et le Cabinet marin - sont situés à l'Est. Par les fenêtres du Cabinet on peut apercevoir Cronstadt, d'un côté, et St.-Pétersbourg de l'autre. Pierre aimait cette pièce. Soulevant la moitié inférieure d'une fenêtre il observait souvent à la longue-vue des mouvements de bateaux sur le golfe de Finlande. Les murs de la Chambre à coucher sont tendus de tissus comme dans les autres palais de Pierre le Grand et le lit a un baldaquin.

Une robe de chambre, un bonnet de nuit sur le lit et une table à braise, une chope en bois, une cruche et un plateau anglais près du lit - ce sont les objets ayant appartenus à Pierre I.

Peu après B.F.Rastrelli ajouta près de Monplaisir des galeries de service et un édifice auquel on donna le nom de Catherine. Catherine II y vivait avant son accession au trône.

**42.** Monplaisir Palace.
Schloß Monplaisir.
Palais de Monplaisir.

**44.** Central Hall.
Großer Saal.
Salle d'apparat.

**43.** Eastern Gallery.
Östliche Galerie.
Galerie d'Est.

**45.** Marine Study.
Marinekabinett Peters I.
Cabinet Marin.

**46.** Bedroom of Peter the Great.
Schlafzimmer Peters I.
Chambre à coucher de Pierre le Grand.

▷
**47.** Catherine Wing.
Katharinen-Trakt  (Katharinenflügel).
Bâtiment de Catherine.

# COTTAGE PALACE

To the east of the Lower Park lies the Alexandria Park housing the building of the Cottage Palace. In contrast to the festive Lower Park filled with noise and splendour, the Alexandria Park breathes peace and quiet. The Alexandria Park was conceived as an Imperial summer villa. In 1829 Emperor Nicholas I made a present of it to his wife Alexandra, after whom the estate was named.

The owners of the estate wanted all the buildings in the Alexandria park to be erected in Gothic style. So the architect Adam Menelas built the Cottage in the English style of Tudor Gothic. The palace is striking due to the harmony of its interiors and dècor.

The most interesting rooms of the ground floor are the Study of the Empress, the Grand and Smaller Reception Halls and the Grand Drawing Room.

Moulded ceilings, chandeliers, mirrors, marble fireplaces, carved furniture, handwoven carpets on the floor - all that combines, in an astonishing way, luxury and homely cosiness. Rich collections of bronze, china and crystal items are gathered in these rooms. Magnificent, is the white china dinner service of 459 pieces displayed in the Dining Hall. It was made at the Imperial factory in St Petersburg. The collection of paintings contains works by the outstanding Russian artists Ivan Aivazovsky, Orest Kiprensky and Sylvestr Shchedrin.

A number of exhibits of the Cottage are not only of artistic value but also of a historical one. One of them is a pair of vases in the Grand Reception Hall made at the Sèvres factory. It was a present of Napoleon to Alexander I while signing the Tilsit Treaties in 1807.

The Cottage Library contains more than 1,000 volumes, mainly works of fiction in German, French and English. The royal family were particularly fond

# SOMMERPALAST COTTAGE

Im Westen des Unteren Parks befindet sich der Landschaftspark *Alexandria* mit dem Sommerpalast *Cottage*. Im Unterschied zu Pracht und Glanz des Unteren Parks herrscht hier Stille und Ruhe. Der *Alexandria* war als Landgut der Zarenfamilie vorgesehen. Im Jahre 1829 schenkte Nikolaus I. dieses Landgut seiner Gemahlin Alexandra, daher die Bezeichnung des ganzen Ensembles.

Nach dem Wunsch der Besitzer sollten alle Bauten im *Alexandria* im gotischen Stil errichtet werden. Darum verwendete der Architekt Adam Menelas bei der Errichtung des Palastes Elemente der englischen, sogenannten Tudor-Gotik. Der Palast überrascht durch die Harmonie der Interieure und deren Einrichtung, die den Eindruck einer einmaligen künstlerischen Einheit vermitteln. Von besonderem Interesse sind die Räume im ersten Geschoß: das *Kabinett* der Zarin, das *Große* und das *Kleine Empfangszimmer* und das *Große Gästezimmer*. Mit Plastikdekor verzierte Decken, Kronleuchter, Spiegel, Marmorkaminen, geschnitzte Möbel, gewebte Teppiche auf dem Boden verbinden erstaunlich die Pracht und die häusliche Gemütlichkeit. In diesen Räumen sind reiche Sammlungen von Gegenständen aus Bronze, Porzellan und Kristall ausgestellt. Prächtig ist das schneeweiße Service aus 459 Teilen, das in der Petersburger Porzellanfabrik hergestellt wurde. Unter den Gemälden sind Werke der hervorragenden russischen Künstler Iwan Aiwasowski, Orest Kiprenski und Semjon Stschedrin.

Einige Gegenstände im Palast sind nicht nur von großem künstlerischem sondern auch von historischem Wert.

# LE COTTAGE

A l'Est du Parc Inférieur s'étend le Parc d'Alexandrie avec le Pavillon du Cottage. Il se distingue du Parc Inférieur plein de bruit et de brillant par son calme et sa quiétude.

L'Alexandrie fut crée comme un domaine de campagne des empereurs. En 1829 Nicolas I l'a offert à sa femme Alexandra d'où son nom.

Selon les désirs de propriétaires tous les édifices d'Alexandrie devaient être bâtis dans le style gothique. Architecte A.Menelas usa des éléments du style gothique anglais dit du Tudor. Le château étonne par l'harmonie des intérieurs et sa décoration qui donne l'impréssion de l'intégrité et l'authenticité artistiques singulières. Les pièces du rez-de-chaussée sont les plus intéressantes: le Cabinet privé de l'impératrice Alexandra, la Grande et la Petite salles de réception, le Grand salon. Les plafonds à moulures, les lustres, les miroirs, les cheminées de marbre, les meubles sculptés, les tapis tissés sur les planchers - tout reunit le luxe et l'ambiance du confort familial d'une manière surprenante. On voit ici des collections riches d'objets de bronze, de porcelaine et de cristal. Dans la Salle à manger un service superbe de 459 pièces realisé à l'usine de porcelaine de Pétersbourg est exposé. La collection de la peinture comporte des tableaux de peintres russes I. Aïvazovski, O. Kiprenski, S. Chtchedrine.

Certaines objets exposés ont non seulement la valeur d'art, mais aussi la grande valeur historique. Ce sont par exemple deux vases magnifiques de Sèvres que Napoléon offrit à Alexandre I à l'occasion de la conclusion de la paix à Tilsit, en 1807.

Le nombre de livres à la Bibliothèque atteint plus de mille volumes, surtout des œuvres littétaires en allemand, francais et anglais parmi lesquels on trouve

of the novels of Sir Walter Scott. An elegant Gothic staircase leads to the upper floors of the Cottage, where the Study of Nicholas I and the chambers of the children are situated. Their dècor is far more austere. The only exception is the Study of the Dowager Empress Maria Fyodorovna, the mother of the last Russian Tsar Nicholas II. The Study was decorated in Art Nouveau style at the end of the 19th century.

Nicholas II used to visit the Alexandria estate up to 1914. On the shore of the Gulf of Finland the so-called Lower Summer House was built for him. It has not survived.

In the years of World War II practically all the palaces and parks of Peterhof were destroyed. It has taken decades of hard work by hundreds of restorers to return the original magnificence to the palaces and parks, these masterpieces of 18th- and 19th-century art.

Die wunderschönen Vasen aus der Sèvres-Manufaktur wurden Alexander I. von Napoleon bei der Unterzeichnung des Friedensvertrages in Tilsit im Jahre 1807 geschenkt.

Die Bibliothek des *Cottages* umfaßt über tausend Bände, hauptsächlich Werke der schöngeistigen Literatur in deutscher, englischer und französischer Sprache. Besonders beliebt waren bei den Bewohnern des Palastes die Romane von Walter Scott.

Eine schön gestaltete gotische Treppe führt in die oberen Geschosse des Cottages. Hier befinden sich das *Kabinett Nikolaus I.* und die *Kinderzimmer*. Ihre Einrichtung erscheint viel strenger und bescheidener. Eine Ausnahme macht das *Kabinett*, das Ende des 19. Jahrhunderts im Jugendstil eingerichtet wurde, das der verwitweten Zarin Maria Fjodorowna, der Mutter des letzten russischen Zaren Nikolaus II. gehörte.

Nikolaus II. benutzte bis 1914 den Alexandria als seine Sommerresidenz. Für ihn wurde ein Sommerhaus, die *Untere Datscha* am Ufer des Finnischen Meerbusens gebaut. Sie ist nicht erhalten geblieben.

In den Jahren des Zweiten Weltkrieges wurde dem ganzen Peterhof-Ensemble ungeheuerer Schaden Zugefügt. Es dauerte Jahrzehnte mühseliger Arbeit von hunderten Restauratoren, bis dieses einmalige Ensemble aus dem 18. und 19. Jahrhundert wieder in seiner ursprünglichen Pracht auferstand.

ceux de W.Scotte préférés des propriétaires impérials.

L'escalier élégant du style gothique mène à l'autre étage du Cottage où se trouvent le Cabinet de travail de Nicolas I et les chambres d'enfants. La décoration des chambres du premier étage est beaucoup plus modeste et austère à l'exception de celle du Cabinet privé de l'impératrice-veuve Maria Fedorovna, la mère du dernier empereur russe Nicolas II. Ce Cabinet fut bâti à la fin du XIXme s. au style moderne.

A propos, le tsar Nicolas II utilisait l'Alexandrie comme sa résidence d'été jusqu'à 1914. On bâtit pour lui la Maison de campagne inférieure qui ne nous est pas parvenue.

Presque tous les palais et parcs de Peterhof ont été victimes de la deuxième guerre mondiale. Le travail obstiné de centaines de restaurateurs fut nécessaire pour restituer cet ensemble majesteux.

**48.** Cottage Palace.
Sommerpalast Cottage.
Cottage.

**49.** *Cottage* Palace.
Marble terrace with the fountain.
Architect A.Stakenschneider, 1842-1843.

Sommerpalast *Cottage.*
Marmorterrasse mit der Fontäne.
Architekt A.Stakenschneider, 1842-1843.

*Cottage.*
Terrasse de marbre avec une fontaine.
Architecte A.Stakenschneider, 1842-1843.

**50.** Smaller Reception Hall.
Kleines Empfangszimmer.
Petite Salle de réception.

**51.** Staircase.
Treppe.
Escalier.

**52.** Dining Room.
Speisezimmer.
Salle à manger.

**53.** Dining Room. Dinner set.
Imperial Porcelain Factory. Russia.

Speisezimmer. Service.
Kaiserliche Porzellanmanufaktur.
Rußland.

Salle à manger. Service.
Usine Impériale de porcelaine. Russie.

**54.** Library.
Bibliothek.
Bibliothèque.

▷
**55.** Grand Drawing Room.
Großes Empfangszimmer.
Grand Salon.

**56.** Study of Nicholas I.
Kabinet Nikolaus I.
Cabinet de travail de Nicolas Ier.